Association Boyd

Proceedings of the

Boyd reunion

Association Boyd

Proceedings of the
Boyd reunion

ISBN/EAN: 9783337732608

Printed in Europe, USA, Canada, Australia, Japan

Cover: Foto ©ninafisch / pixelio.de

More available books at **www.hansebooks.com**

PROCEEDINGS

--of--

THE SIXTH

BOYD REUNION,

HELD AT

MARION, OHIO,

(HOTEL MARION,)

August 27th and 28th, 1890.

YOUNGSTOWN, O.:
H. BYNES, BOOK AND JOB PRINTER.
1892

Boyd Association Publications.

1. THE FAMILY RECORD. Printed for framing. Contains all the names of the fourth generations of the Boyd kin. *Price* ... rge card suitable ... econd, third and ... *er copy.*

2. Proceedings of Beaver Reunion in 1... information regarding the initial Reunion about, and all the addresses and poems del matters of interest. *Price, 15 cents per cop*... Contains valuable ...w it was brought there, with other

3. Proceedings of Lima Reunion in 188... Contains the first Constitution of the Assoc... of the second gathering of the Boyds. *Pr*... 8-page pamphlet. with a full report *ents per copy.*

4. Proceedings of Kiskminister Reunio... contains important Biographical sketches. ... 4. 36 pages, and , *20 cents.*

5. Proceedings of Hamilton Reunion in... esting history. *Price, 20 cents.* ... 32 pages of inter-

6. Proceedings of Pittsburg Reunion ... full report of the largest gathering, addr... reports. *Price, 25 cents.* ... . 60 pages, with nd sketches, with

7. Proceedings of Marion Reunion in 1... Committee on Incorporation, with propose and sketch of M. Hillis Boyd. *Price, 25* ... Contains report of titution, addresses

Any of these publications will be se... application to the Secretary at Poulan, Georgia.

—OF—

THE SIXTH

BOYD REUNION,

HELD AT

MARION, OHIO,

(HOTEL MARION,)

August 27th and 28th, 1890.

———•◦•———

YOUNGSTOWN, O.:
H. BYXBE, BOOK AND JOB PRINTER.
1892.

THE BOYD ASSOCIATION.

OFFICERS.

REV. T. S. NEGLEY..........................PRESIDENT.
    KENNETH, PA.

H. STEELE SMITH, ESQ..................VICE PRESIDENT.
    FREEPORT, PA.

DR. J. F. WILSON......................SEC'Y AND TREAS.
    POULAN, GA.

DR. GEO. J. BOYD......................ASSISTANT SEC'Y.
    BLACK HAWK, PA.

COMMITTEE OF ARRANGEMENTS FOR REUNION OF 1892.

H. STEELE SMITH, Freeport, Pa. DR. GEO. J. BOYD, Black Hawk, Pa.
H. H. NEGLEY, Pittsburgh, Pa. A. HILLIS BOYD, Allegheny, Pa.
  MRS. MARY B. McKOWN, Pittsburgh, Pa.

HISTORICAL COMMITTEE.

REV. J. H. SHIELDS, CHAIRMAN. C. N. BOYD, ESQ.
MRS. S. A. HENRY.   REV. J. S. BOYD.
HON. F. A. BOYD.   MISS CLARA McCONNELL.
W. H. LEARD, ESQ.   MRS. JULIA A. SCOTT.
MRS. S. C. BERRYMAN.   MR. ROBERT G. BOYD.

TRUSTEES.

ROBERT G. BOYD, Marion, O...................Term expires 1890.
JAMES F. WILSON, Poulan, Ga..................... " " 1890.
A. FULTON BOYD, Poland, Ohio.................... " " 1892.
R. D. HUMES, West Newton, Pa................... " " 1892.
J. F. BOYD, Chambersburg, Pa.................... " " 1894.
CHAS. N. BOYD, Butler, Pa....................... " " 1894.

PREFATORY.

These pages come to the Boyd kin through many trials and much tribulation. Your Secretary, in view of his removal to the South, declined a re-election at the Pittsburgh Reunion in 1888, but *the work* "clings to him still," and he is content to continue his humble services while they seem to be appreciated. His necessary absence from the Marion Reunion, and the failure of an express company to promptly deliver an important package, was the occasion of much disappointment to those in attendance, and caused the delaying until next meeting of much important business.

Matters also of particular interest were lying in the Marion post-office during the entire session of the Reunion, and although directed in care of the "Hotel Marion," were not delivered, but subsequently returned to the sender.

Much of the matter contained in this pamphlet has not been before the Marion Reunion for the reasons previously mentioned, and as far as the new constitution is concerned, it is embodied in order that the friends may have an opportunity to know its character, and act intelligently when it comes up for adoption at the next meeting.

It may appear to some of the friends, that there is unnecessary delay in issuance of this pamphlet. However, late as it now appears, it is still in advance of more than enough delinquent dues of members to cover its cost of publication. The work has not been delayed—particularly on this account, but rather from the fact that a large and exacting business requires the constant attention of your Secretary, during the full day, while a voluminous correspondence and the book-keeping his business requires, necessitates a second day's amount of labor every night.

The work is now pushed to completion, during a few days of convalescence following a slight indisposition, which necessitated an omission, for a time, of regular duties.

J. F. WILSON,
Secretary.

POULAN, GA., May 2d, 1892.

ADDRESS OF WELCOME.

[BY WINONA H. HUGHES, MARION, O.]

From the south of Europe, in that sea-indented land so rich in classic lore, the stories of the "guest-friendships of Homeric days," as unchangeable as the Grecian mountains in whose shadows these friendships were formed, are handed down to us as shining examples of genuine welcome and hospitality. Very slight was the bond which first united the stranger to his host. The mere fact that he was a stranger was sufficient ground for the host to bring forth the best the house afforded and place before him. And having once partaken of food together their lasting friendship was sealed.

But we are bound by a stronger tie than the fact that many of us are strangers. We are united by the ties of kinship; we belong to the same family; and this friendship of kin is cemented by the bonds of christian sympathy and love.

In the strength of these ties, we greet you, and warmly welcome you into our midst and gladly extend the hand of welcome to all the friends here assembled.

We are glad that we belong to this family, whose history we can trace back to the sturdy, God-fearing people who dwelt among the rolling hills of Northern Ireland. To this day the people of that far-away spot are held as shining examples of industry and sturdy piety; and those who left their native clime lost none of those sterling qualities when they came to the rugged wilds of the new country. Rather their piety increased as the distance from the Green Isle of Erin increased, until all over this land, in almost every State, the godly influence of the Boyds is felt. At every Reunion, the virtue and piety of our ancestors, and more particularly of ourselves, are extolled, and rightly so.

However, it might be well for us, at such times as this, to call to mind for an instant the fact, that the Boyds are not the only people in existence. There are Joneses in the world and likewise Smiths, an innumerable host. And so long as the fact remains that the Smiths and Joneses are not myths, the Boyds can not claim the earth.

Yet, acknowledging all our greatness, all our smartness, and especially our goodness, we may profitably consider how we can better even our present state. Here an especial opportunity is

presented for cultivating and uplifting every faculty of the soul. "Iron sharpeneth iron; so a man sharpeneth the countenance of his friend." In this concourse of people every intellect may receive a new impulse, a fresh inspiration for lofty ideals, and each soul, as it returns to its accustomed routine of duties, may go with the will firmly determined to have a more varied surface over which the intellect may roam.

However much we may crave knowledge or intellectual growth, there is yet a more important soul faculty to be cared for. As the heart of Ethan Brand was turned to stone because every other noble feeling and impulse was crowded therefrom by the one absorbing passion for knowledge, so, on the contrary, our warmest feelings and tenderest emotions may be stirred and enlarged by this mingling of friends. For, as our noble Emerson says, "Every soul is a celestial Venus to every other soul. The heart has its sabbaths and jubilees in which the world appears as a hymeneal feast."

Each reunion may be made a sabbattical period, a jubilee in the soul's experience. Feelings of joy flood the hearts as the hands of friends long separated are clasped, and the soul is refreshed and uplifted by touching again the soul once so familiar, for "the best part of friendship remains untouched by time and circumstances." Nor are the new friendships formed less conducive to soul growth than the renewal of old ones. And, to quote again, "Every promise of the soul has innumerable fulfillments; each of its joys ripens into a new want." Here, while our souls are glowing with joy and pleasure, we turn our grateful thoughts to him so lately taken from us, who was the instigator of these meetings. I refer to M. Hillis Boyd. In starting this movement he must have had in mind the great pleasure to be derived from it. And from each of these joys ripening into a new want, every soul is impelled to satisfy this want by striving to attain the ideal type of humanity in which all the powers are developed, yet subject to the higher power of a will molded after the Infinite. And as we welcome this assembled family to-day, it is with the hope that each of us may receive not only the full measure of fleeting joy, but also that each of us may make a few strides forward in that soul growth and culture which blossoms into the perfect love toward God.

JAMES BROWN AND AGNES (NANCY) BROWN.

MAY 6TH, 1830.—MAY 6TH, 1890.

[BY REV. J. F. BOYD, STEUBENVILLE, OHIO.]

Dear father, mother, we have come,
   On this your festal day,
To greet you in the dear old home,
   And love's fond tribute pay.

The day you did each other mate,
   Just sixty years ago,
Its scenes and joys could you relate,
   We would be pleased to know.

But you may say we all but one
   Have passed the "honey moon,"
And by experience best is known
   Life's morning, night and noon.

They are but few, whose wedded life
   Has passed through three-score years
Of joy, of grief, of toil and strife,
   Of comforts, hopes and fears.

And could we all our lives compare
   With yours of long ago,
And trace each down with strictest care,
   A difference wide 'twould show.

In many ways—in length of time—
   Great changes all around,
In church and state, in every clime,
   The skeptical confound.

And should a like advance be made
   In sixty years to come,
In science, art, of every grade,
   Who'd dare to count the sum?

We therefore most devoutly pray
   All may devoted be,
To usher in th' Millenial day,
   The world's grand jubilee.

We know you have not lived in vain;
   The good which you have done
Cannot be told till all shall gain
   That home beyond the sun.

From beauteous springs on mountain side,
   Two sparkling streams flow down,
Until they meet and form one tide—
   A river now is shown.

With wider, deeper force it flows
   Down thro' the spreading vale,
'Midst flowery meads, its beauty grows
   Till lost 'mid Ocean's wail,

So may your life flow calmly on,
   'Mid blessings from above;
Till done with earth, and you have won
   The ocean of God's love.

"The single one," her life has been
   So useful, who can tell?
In church and parents' home 'tis seen,
   And for us all 'tis well.

We doubt not, many yet will rise
   And call her blessed, too;
Without her help here to devise,
   Not much the rest could do.

Five daughters and a worthy son,
   On earth, enjoy God's grace,
While seven, in all, their race have run.
   Now see God's smiling face.

Two sons, two daughters, God did call
   In life's fair, beauteous morn,
To where no ill can them befall,
   And two quite soon as born.

One son was spared and loved by all,
   A loving wife had he,
And children four, when God did call,
   "Come higher, dwell with me."

His faith was strong, he had no fear;
   To him death had no sting,
Except to leave his family dear,
   Whom he to Christ did bring.

In prayer and faith, and now they all
   Are in the Shepherd's fold ;
We trust they'll share, at Jesus' call,
   Joys that can ne'er be told.

One son-in-law, by all beloved,
   Brief sickness called away ;
In midst of usefulness removed,
   We trust, to endless day.

Grand-children, twenty-three, in all,
   Of whom sixteen remain,
While seven, quite young, did hear the call,
   Eternal life did gain.

And one grand-son, by marriage, called
   Of God, he quickly died ;
His wife and parents stood appalled —
   She lately was a bride.

How quick the transit ! who can tell,
   To Heaven's golden shore ?
To us a shock !—with him 'tis well,
   And will be evermore.

The darkest clouds, could we but see
   Upon the upper side,
How bright and beautiful 'twould be !
   That time let us abide.

Our tenderest sympathies do flow
   To those bereft, to-day.
May God His richest grace bestow,
   And light their future way !

Eight great-grand-children you can boast,
   Three you have never seen ;
And their grand-mothers think, almost,
   Their equals ne'er have been.

Your prayers and teachings God did bless
   Unto your children dear ;
That all did early Christ confess —
   This should your spirits cheer.

Grand-children, too, as you well know,
   Of young and tender years,
In this respect, like spirit show ;
   Thus covenant grace appears.

Of those dear friends who saw the scene
   We celebrate to-day,
How many years do intervene
   Since they were called away ?

They with your children gone before,
   And all our kindred dear,
Now gathered on the heavenly shore--
   Their songs we almost hear.

How sweet to view them waiting there,
   Arrayed in garments white,
And looking down, with vision rare
   And feelings of delight.

O blessed hope ! We all may meet
   Where ill can never come,
And greatest festal celebrate,
   In that eternal home.

FULTON HISTORY.

KEOKUK, IOWA, Aug. 22d, 1890.

J. F. WILSON, Esq., Poulan, Ga.:

My Dear Sir:

Your letter of the 30th ult. to Rev. J. S. Boyd, La Moure, North Dakota, requesting him to prepare a brief sketch of *"Fulton Notes and Notables,"* has been forwarded me with the request to prepare the paper desired. In answer I wrote to him the *theme* was too barren, and even if it were not, I was too busy to prepare a paper worthy to be read before your Association—a body containing so many learned men. But Cousin Boyd has replied in a second letter, urging the matter and asking that I would give you some of the items given in rather a desultory way in my hurried letter to him. In compliance I will do so, and this rather prosy explanation must be my apology for addressing you this letter without an official invitation thereto.

One item of "Fulton" history I presume would interest the "Boyds," as it equally concerns both tribes, viz., the "Habitat" or precise locality of our common ancestry, the home in Ireland of *"Abraham Fulton, his wife and family."* These were the parents of your maternal ancestor, Mary Fulton Boyd, whose brothers, Abraham, James, Robert, Henry and Joseph, and sister Margaret, were the ancestors of the Fultons and Irvins, known as the "Fultons" of our lineage.

I enclose you herewith a copy of the church letter brought by this Abraham Fulton from Ireland, dated 1772. He was my Great Grand-Father. His son Robert my Grand-Father. The letter has been treasured in my father's (Wm. Fulton) family, and as the sole surviving member of the family it is my good fortune to be its custodian, as well as that of an old needle-worked pocket book brought with it from Ireland.

This letter has at last been the means of conclusively identifying the exact locality of the church granting it, and of the identity of signers of the document. The church or congregation is known in Ireland at the present day as *Dunboe 1st.* The place named "Articlave" is a small hamlet or locality not given on the maps. The location is on the extreme north of Ireland, at the mouth of the river Bann, about twelve miles west of the Giants' Causeway.

The church is still a strong and prosperous one, and now and since July 26, 1867, has been under the ministration of Rev. John Mark, with whom I have had some exceedingly interesting correspondence. I know I cannot write you anything more interesting than to copy herein certain extracts from one or two of his letters to me, promising that on the back of the certificate enclosed my daughter has copied a history of this *Dunboe Church*, which identifies the certificate, etc., the certificate and history on back thereof being needed to fully understand these extracts.

COPY OF REV. JOHN MARK'S LETTER.

Nov. 11, 1889.   DUNBOE MANSE, CASTLEROCK CO.,
LONDONDERRY, IRELAND.

Dear Friend: Although we have never met in life, and never may meet, yet I feel that there is much in common between us that I am justified in calling you my "friend." It is refreshing in these times of worldliness and self-seeking to find a man so interested in his ancestry. It is cheering also amidst the ups and downs of social life to find a race steadfastly true to the faith of their fathers, and that through so many generations, and in a land like America, where the population is so shifting and changes so common. I rejoice that amidst the activities of life you take such a deep interest in church life and work, and so promote the glory of your fathers' God in sustaining and extending the kingdom of His dear Son on the earth. * * * * I received your letter with no little curiosity, * * * and since its reception I have been diligent in seeking information from some of our oldest inhabitants in relation to those points in your letter which seemed to be of most interest to you. The first minister of Dunboe was one *Thomas Fulton*, and as far as I can discover your ancestors were either descendants of said Thomas Fulton or fellow-colonists, who came with him to Ireland and settled here somewhere about 1660. They possessed the town-land of Bellyquitlan, a tract of land lying in the angle formed by the River Baun, flowing into the Atlantic ocean. From this home they have passed away almost a century ago, and their town-land is now owned and occupied by four families, all called "Dugan" by name. The last of the Fultons was a woman married to a man called "Clarke." They lived in the town-land of Exorna, and occupied the house built by the Rev. Robert Knox, minister of Dunboe, who died in 1746. They, too, have passed away. Your family is now extinct. We have other Fultons, but they are not of your lineage. In this town-land of Exorna, *Robert Guthrie* lived, who signed your ancestors' certificate (a copy of which* you have so kindly sent me and which I shall treasure) and his great-great-grandson now lives in the old ancestral house. His name is Robert Guthrie. He is one of the oldest and most honored citizens and is an Elder in the church of 1st Dunboe. His father's name was James Guthrie, and James' father was Robert Guthrie, who signed said certificate in 1772. The present Robert Guthrie has a *Margaret Guthrie* in

---

*See page 17, Proceedings of Hamilton Reunion.

his family, and also two sons, called respectively James and Benjamin, so you see the old names are still preserved from generation to generation and perpetuated down the centuries. It seems the tradition in your family is correct, namely, that Abraham Fulton, who emigrated to America in 1772, was married to a sister of Robert Guthrie, who, as Elder, signed the church certificate of the said Abraham Fulton. You will thus see that while your family by your paternal ancestor is extinct, yet by the side of your maternal ancestor it is still with us ; and there are no more worthy or honored people, whether viewed as citizens or church men. My nearest neighbor is a Mr. Thomas Henry, whose mother was a Margaret. Guthrie (sister to our present Robert Guthrie) and he is an honored and energetic Elder in the church of which I am minister, and to him I am largely indebted for the information which this letter contains. Any old thing possesses a charm for him. His desire is to be among the tombs, and to gather and treasure up old relics of the past. He has a very tenacious memory, so that he seems never to forget anything he has ever heard. Indeed, from reading your letter, which to me was deeply interesting, and gathering up from it what I could of the spirit and motives which characterize your family in America, I have come to the conclusion that you have many things in common with your friends in the Old Country. I presume we all inherit as much or more from our mothers than from our fathers, and so the blood and spirit of your maternal ancestors seem to have flowed down the generations and still to be perpetuating itself on both sides of the Atlantic. * * * * * *

I am pleased to hear from you of family reunions. May the spirit that prompted them live and thrive. "Why should auld acquaintance be forgot, etc. ?" Such reunions open up channels along which the milk of human kindness may flow freely. I am delighted to learn that the great majority of your kindred are children of the "Auld Kirk," as they say in Scotland.

Let me in conclusion pray that you and yours may be heirs of all the "covenant blessings" for time and eternity. God bless you.

I remain,

Yours most sincerely,
JOHN MARK.

WM. FULTON, ESQ.,
  KEOKUK.

If it would not weary you, I could write how this said correspondence was rather singularly and almost romantically varied about a month ago by a cablegram from Mr. Mark, saying, "Visit immediately Aberdeen, Dakota, and preserve property," &c., &c., to which I responded the following day, and spent a very delightful "outing" of almost 700 miles travel through Northern Iowa, Dakota and Minnesota, and as many returning, "preserving" quite a considerable estate to which *Mrs.* Mark had fallen heir by the death of an uncle of whose varied wanderings his friends had known but little for many years. Since my return, a few days ago, I received a long letter from Mr. Mark, explaining more fully his cable-

gram, which closed with the following warm Irish welcome should I ever visit the old country:

"* * * * * * I do hope you and I may yet be spared to meet in "life—perhaps in America, but better still in 'old Ireland.' If you can at "any time find it convenient to take a run over we will be happy should "you make your home with us during your stay. You can then visit the "cradle of your ancestors, see the old homesteadings and make the ac- "quaintance of your people, all of whom will be glad to see you, though "many generations lie between. I need say no more. God bless you and "make you a blessing.
"Believe me to remain,
"Faithfully Yours,
"JOHN MARK."
"WM. FULTON, Esq.,
"Keokuk, Iowa, U. S. A."

You will find in comparing the date of church certificate "1772" with the date of the pastorate of Rev. Wm. Knox, whose name is appended to certificate, which pastorate began in 1765 and ended August, 1801, that it covers the date of letter 1772, showing as a matter of evidence that dates *synchronize* and prove each other. That the church at that date was of some standing is shown by this Rev. Wm. Knox coming there from "Mary's Abbey, Ireland," which, I believe, is the church that Rev. Dr. John Hall, of New York, left when he was called to New York. Mr. Mark, the present pastor, and who writes me, I notice by the Belfast *Witness*, was a prominent speaker in the Presbyterian convention that met in Ireland this summer.

In behalf of the "Fultons" I congratulate the "Boyds" that we together have the satisfaction of knowing that we have descended from a race whose history we need not fear to record, and whatever laudable pride we may have in running it back the 230 years we have, and there finding it either merged in a Presbyterian minister or a co-colonist of one who was a "Pioneer" even in that ancient country, can be shared equally by both the Boyd and Fulton branches; and that the covenant made with the ancient Abraham of old, that his seed should be as the sands of the sea or stars of the heavens as to number, must have been reflected on the devout prayers made by our common ancestor, Abraham Fulton, wife and family, when they "went to God in prayer" before deciding to embark on what was then a great journey to a new country.

But I fear I weary you. Cousin Boyd had two heads or topics for me to write on: 1st, "Fulton notes," which I have already done;

2d, "Fulton Notables." The latter can easily and speedily be disposed of, and in the same manner that St. Patrick or some other historian of Ireland wrote the celebrated chapter on the "Snakes" of that island, viz.: "Chapter 2d—Snakes. There are no snakes in Ireland." Imitating his compactness of style, I will write—

Chapter 2d—Fulton Notables.
There are no Fulton Notables.

Yours very truly,

WM. FULTON.

HISTORY OF DUNBOE 1st.

The *first minister* of Dunboe is said to have been *Mr. Thomas Fulton*, who was here in *1660*. He appears to have been succeeded by Mr. Blair, but of his ministry nothing is now known with certainty. The next minister was Mr. John Wilson, who was here in 1684. He fled to Scotland in the troublous times which preceded the Revolution, and settled at Largs. The Presbytery of Irwin in 1691 supplicated for his removal from Dunboe, but the Synod of Ulster refused to accede to the proposal. He continued, notwithstanding, to remain in Scotland, and at length, in 1697, the Synod yielded, and he was formally installed at Largs. After this, a Mr. Woodside appears for some time to have ministered to the people. In October, 1719, Mr. Robert Knox was ordained to the ministry in this congregation. Mr. Knox died here on the 1st of April, 1746. The next minister was Mr. Wm. Cochrane, who was ordained here on the 10th of May, 1748. In 1762, Mr. Cochrane resigned his charge and conformed to the Established Church. He was succeeded by *Mr. Wm. Knox*, who was installed here on the *18th of August, 1765*. Mr. Knox had *previously been minister of St. Mary's Abbey, Dublin*. Mr. Knox died here on the *29th of August, 1801*, and a stone inserted in a conspicuous position in the front wall of the place of his burial still bears honorable testimony to the excellence of his character. His descendants, in good worldly circumstances, are still to be found in the neighborhood of Coleraine; but with the exception of the family of the late Mr. Mark, of Castlerock, they no longer adhere to the Presbyterian Church. The next minister was Mr. Thomas Greer, who was ordained here on the 9th of March, 1802. Among his descendants are the Rev. Thomas Greer, of Anahilt, and the late S. M. Greer, Esq., Recorder of Derry, and at one time M. P. for the County. Mr. Greer died here on the 15th of December, 1812, and was succeeded by Mr. Wm. Lyle, who was ordained here on the 7th of June, 1814. Mr. Lyle died on the 3rd of April, 1867, and was succeeded by *Mr. John Mark, who was ordained here on the 24th of July of the same year*.

[Copied from History of Congregations of the Presbyterian Church in Ireland, by Rev. W. D. Killen, D.D. Published by James Cleeland, Belfast.]

FAMILY HISTORY.

[BY MRS. S. C. BERRYMAN.]

THE FAMILY OF HENRY AND MARGARET BOYD.

The children of this family were James, John, Abraham, Fulton and Mary. They organized as a family in March, 1804, and flourished for the most part on the "Western Reserve." James died in 1867. His children, three sons and three daughters, are living in Illinois, Kansas and Wisconsin.

John lives upon his farm in Allen county, Ohio, with his only surviving daughter. His aged companion passed away Jan. 18th, 1889. There has been one marriage and one birth among his children's children since the last reunion.

Abraham has suffered the loss, by death, of his beloved daughter Mary and his daughter-in-law Ellen. His only son, with his motherless children, have removed to a ranch in the vicinity of Sherman, Lincoln county, Washington. Abraham lives with his only surviving daughter on the farm he reclaimed from the wilderness, near Lima, Ohio, and is enjoying a peaceful, happy old age: active and helpful in the home and in his beloved church, both having grown under his watchful, fostering care. There is one birth to report, that of the first great-grandchild, whose name is Ethel Boyd Kemper.

Mary, the only daughter of Henry and Margaret Boyd, passed away so gently that the loving watchers by her side scarce knew when her spirit took its flight. The daughter at whose home she died, in Palmyra, Ohio, wrote thus: "The struggle was sharp but mercifully short, hardly two hours; but oh! the vacancy in our hearts and homes. But the blessed Comforter soon spake and said, 'There is rejoicing in Heaven this morning. Father, Grandfather and Grandmother are saying, Mary has come; and the Redeemer is saying, Well done, good and faithful servant.' As the circle narrows on earth it widens in Heaven." Dr. Wilson, our efficient and popular "scribe" and Mary's only son, has removed to the Sunny South since last reunion. He traversed over a thousand miles to be present the Sabbath afternoon, Sept. 1st, 1889, when a

large concourse of old friends gathered at the old church at North Benton to lay his mother's precious dust by the side of that of her husband, which had lain there nearly twenty years.

Henry Fulton, the younger son of this family, lives near Lincoln, Nebraska, on a farm, and is actively engaged, with his wife and two young sons and three daughters, in agricultural pursuits. His is the distinction of having the next to the longest list of sons and daughters on our family record, he having been the father of 14 children. There has only been one accession to this branch of the family, but the little one died after a few short weeks.

Fulton has two sons living in Kansas, whom he has not seen for many years. A short time ago he determined to make them a visit and to surprise them by going unannounced. It was the unexpected that happened in this case. They knew him instantly, but it was with the greatest difficulty that he could be brought to realize that they were his sons.

The sum of the ages of this family of seven is 542 years, giving an average of 77.4.

There have been five deaths, one marriage and three births since last report.

SKETCH OF M. HILLIS BOYD.

[BY REV. A. FULTON BOYD.]

DIED.—July 10th, 1890, at his home, near Freeport, Pa., M. HILLIS BOYD.

The subject of this notice was born March 14th, 1842. He was the second son of Abram and Mary Boyd. He was an invalid for some thirty years. When but a boy he received internal injuries from an unmanageable horse, from which he never fully recovered. He lived on the farm with his parents until in the time of our country's great need he enlisted in her service, September 9th, 1862, and remained with his company until the close of the war.

After his return from the army he was married to Miss Lizzie F. Dunaway, of Merrittstown, Pa., and they began housekeeping at the old home, father and mother having moved to Slate Lick, Pa. But the trials and exposures of army life were too much for his feeble frame, producing throat and lung trouble, which finally resulted in his death.

When about eighteen years of age he became a member in full communion of the Presbyterian church of Slate Lick, Pa. He retained his membership there until the organization, in 1871, of the Shrader Grove church, at which time he was elected Elder and served in that capacity until the time of his death.

For a number of years he was leader in the Service of Song, first in the church at Slate Lick and afterwards at Shrader Grove.

He was an earnest Christian worker, as was truly said at his funeral service, "He knew no life but a religious life." He, with his family, worshipped God every morning and evening. He was very careful in the religious training of his children, and often talked with the writer of this notice about the covenant relation of children and the duty of Christian parents, desiring to fully understand the teaching of God's Word upon those subjects, that he might be enabled to bring up his loved ones in the nurture and admonition of the Lord. He was also a faithful servant of God in the Sabbath school. He was Superintendent of Shrader Grove Sabbath school most of the time before and since the organization of the church. But his special work in the Sabbath school was as a teacher. He always felt that God called upon him to save every unregenerated member of his class. He was so conscientious in this matter and so earnest that it was once said of him, "He would have a class but a short time until all were converted." He was loved by all his Sabbath school scholars. At one time it was thought best that he should take a new class for the purpose of interesting some who were not regular in attendance. The class was formed and he took charge of it, but his former class all came into it and would not consent to be deprived of his teaching. He was a wise counsellor in all church matters and

a liberal contributor, not only to the home church but to all the missionary and benevolent works of the General Assembly.

Next to the church and his family were his friends. Friends were always welcome to "Uncle Abram's," and no one gave them a more hearty welcome than Brother Hillis. This trait of character is well illustrated in what he has done for the Boyd Family. He began corresponding with Mr. R. G. Boyd, of Marion, Ohio ; Mr. Abram Boyd, of Lima, Ohio ; Dr. J. F. Wilson, then of Youngstown, Ohio, and others, in regard to looking up the history of the family in the hope that some kind of an organization might be formed which would preserve the history of the entire family, strengthen the family tie and make us more zealous to carry out the desire of our ancestors, to preserve a seed to serve the Lord.

In this effort he was encouraged by all the friends ; and one of the greatest pleasures of his life was to see the family assembled in convention time after time, until a permanent organization was effected to preserve our history.

He spent two years in searching for the different members of the Boyd Family before the record was complete. He was sometimes compelled to write three or four letters before he could get a reply from friends who knew nothing about him and did not suppose that he was one of their kin. As correspondence increased he would often write until near midnight, after a hard day's work on the farm, answering queries of friends. This work was a pleasure to him. He said it was made pleasant by the many kind and encouraging letters received from the friends in answer to his inquiries.

But when his part of the work was done, the organization effected and the work divided among the different branches of the family, he said his heart was too full for utterance, when the friends in convention assembled manifested their appreciation of his endeavors in the presentation to him of a handsome gold watch with this inscription :

M. HILLIS BOYD,
FROM
THE BOYD FAMILY,
LIMA, OHIO,
OCT. 25TH, 1883.

It may be interesting to the friends to know that in his last will and testament he bequeathed the watch to his son Joseph *Hillis* Boyd, to be kept by him and his descendants in the Boyd Family forever.

He looked forward with pleasure to the Reunions, but now *his history* is to be recorded. He has gone to attend the *Grand Reunion*. His record as a soldier has already been written and will be published in its proper place.

In his life he was an obedient son, an affectionate brother, a loving and faithful husband, a kind and indulgent father, in the true sense of these words. Those who knew him best loved him most. As we look over his life we can see but little to condemn. We are grateful to God for his life on earth, grateful for what he was to us, grateful for what he was to others, and even now, in the midst of our sorrow, we rejoice in his death.

Do we not, more than ever before, grasp the meaning of those sweet words of Holy Writ: "Precious in the sight of the Lord is the death of His saints"? He was one of the Lord's jewels. He lived a noble life and died a triumphant death, and why should we not rejoice that he has gone to be with the Lord? He is not dead, but sleepeth, and while we mourn his loss we await the Lord's call to meet him at the *Great Reunion* when our joy will be *full and everlasting*.

The last words he wrote for the Boyd family are the names and dates of friends departed since our last Reunion, and were he to speak to you in conversation to-day his advice would be, in the words written at the head of the list of the dead, sent in his own hand—"*Be ye also ready.*"

REPORT OF COMMITTEE—RESOLUTIONS ON DEATH OF M. HILLIS BOYD.

It has pleased the All-Wise to remove from our association on earth to the reunion above, the soul of our friend and brother in kindred bonds, M. Hillis Boyd. His undying spirit now chants praises in the choir that surrounds the Great White Throne; his form shall rest beneath the clods of the valley till the notes of the last trump shall be raised incorruptible. Though he has passed through the gates of death, his influence cannot die; his life has been to us a noble example. He has shown how beautiful our lives may be and how powerful for good, when they are the expressions of brotherly love sanctified by the love of Christ.

To him we owe the pleasure derived from these reunions, and although his face will be with us no more, the remembrance of his noble manhood will be cherished in our hearts and his influence will continue in the lives of his brethren.

As a feeble expression of the sorrow that veils our hearts, we would say to his bereaved family: We loved him much, you loved him more; our hearts are sad, yours are sadder. We commend you in your affliction to the God whose it is to give and take away, and above all who will keep in perfect peace those whose minds are on Him, because they trusted in Him.

With love for the departed one, and sympathy for his bereaved family, this memorial is placed on record.
ABBY HILL,
S. C. BERRYMAN,
KATE MINTON,
Committee.

ON THE DEATH OF COUSIN M. H. BOYD, FREEPORT, PA.

BY REV. J. F. BOYD.

Another loved friend has gone,
And joined the throng around the throne;
The loss to church, and family dear,
Cannot be fully reckoned here.

To him, we feel assured, 'tis gain;
Beyond all sorrow, toil and pain,
He dwells secure in mansions bright,
Arrayed in robes of matchless white.

With crown of gold upon his brow,
He bears the palm of victory now;
O'er all the powers of earth and hell,
His joys so great no tongue can tell.

With all the dear ones gone before,
He's joined our Savior to adore,
From golden harp to sound His praise,
In sweetest notes, thro' endless days.

Who would not wish to join that throng,
Unite in highest, sweetest song,
To Him who saves us by his blood,
And makes kings and priests to God?

O may that Friend be yours and mine,
With all His love and power divine—
With all our powers Him serve in love,
Then all His glory share above.

What a "Reunion" there will be!
Beyond what mortal eye can see!
May we, with all our kindred dear,
That last and best "Reunion" share!!

OBITUARIES.

[Since the death of the Secretary of the Historical Committee, the chronology of the family has received much less attention than it demands. Reports are manifestly incomplete, particularly as to Births and Marriages, as but one branch of the family has reported any for this pamphlet.
J. F. W.]

DIED—Jan. 16th, 1889, BENNIE, aged 24 days, beloved son of Wm. S. and Julia Boyd, at their home in Baldwin City, Kansas.

DIED—March 17th, 1889, near Rochester, Ind., ELLEN, beloved wife of Henry E. Boyd. The circumstances surrounding this death were peculiarly trying. They had sold their farm and her husband had gone to Washington to seek a home, to which he expected to remove his family as soon as practicable. A fortnight after his departure she was taken violently ill with typhoid pneumonia and died within a week. Four little children, the elder, Nellie, aged twelve; the younger, Maggie Beer, a sweet child of three, were left desolate indeed. Her husband returned and marked her lonely grave by a simple stone and took the little ones, motherless, to the far western home. She was a fond and tender wife and mother.

ANN LAZARUS BOYD.

Ann Lazarus Boyd was born in Deerfield, Portage Co., Ohio, Jan. 26, 1811. Her grandfather, John Hartzell, was instrumental in building up the Presbyterian church at Deerfield. He was inspired by a sermon preached in the neighborhood by Rev. Jas. Boyd, of sainted memory. She united with this church in her youth. March 16th, 1837, she was married to John Boyd. The early years of their married life were spent on a farm near Deerfield and their four children were born there. In 1854 she, with her family, removed to Allen county and settled upon a farm four miles from Lima, where the remainder of her life was spent. She was one of the mothers whose heart-breaking privilege it was to give up the son—the only one—to her country. He enlisted in the 99th O. V. I. in 1862 and only served a few weeks ere his body was brought home and laid to rest in our peaceful "grave yard." Two daughters preceded her to the "home over there" in quick succession, while she herself was an invalid and patiently awaiting the final summons, which came Jan. 18, 1889. She was patient and cheerful and bore the many afflictions with Christian resignation and passed away peacefully one week before her 79th birthday. Her aged companion and one daughter are all of her immediate family that remain to mourn.

DIED—At Palmyra, O., Aug, 29th, 1889, MRS. MARY WILSON, aged 75 years, 5 months and 9 days. Mary was the only daughter of Henry and Margaret (Beer) Boyd, and was born in Ellsworth, Ohio, March 20, 1814. Her

parents had then been in Ohio about two years. Three brothers older and one younger than herself constituted the family. The mother being a delicate woman, the labors and cares incident to pioneer life were laid upon her in her early years. In 1833 the family removed to the adjoining township, Berlin, Mahoning county, and settled on the farm on which she spent the greater portion of her life, within the bounds of what was then called Deerfield, but now North Benton, Presbyterian Church. She was married October 22, 1840, to Joseph Wilson, of Salem, Ohio. She united with the church in early life and ever adorned her profession. She was the worthy daughter of her godly parents. After nearly twenty years of widowhood she was suddenly called to go up higher on the early morning of August 29th, 1889.

DIED—April 16th, 1889, in Shawnee, at the old Boyd homestead, MARY, beloved wife of J. W. Black and youngest daughter of Abram and Maria Hover Boyd. Mary was born May 18, 1849, near the same spot where her life went out almost 40 years later. Here her childhood was passed and here she was married Sept. 14, 1871. Most of her married life was spent in Lima until failing health in both husband and wife caused them to feel that a change was desirable.

They went first to Colorado and then to Rochester, Ind., where they lived four years, forming many pleasant friendships and associations. But disease had an unyielding hold upon her and as the end drew near, her heart yearned for the old father, old home and old friends. Arrangements were accordingly made and time set for returning home, but there was still a work for them to do in Indiana. Her brother's wife sickened and in one short week died, leaving four small children to look to Mr. and Mrs. Black for home and care, their father being absent in the far West. But the cares of life, the sore need of motherless children could no longer detain her. She felt that she was sinking fast and with unwavering desire to die at home she made the weary journey eight days before she died. To her it was a great pleasure to meet the many friends who called to see her. She could not talk much, but for all she had a pleasant smile. Loving hands and sad hearts ministered to her few earthly needs and went with her to the very verge of the valley of the shadow of death. She was not loth to go, having been a member of the church militant, she felt confident of an abundant entrance into the church triumphant. A great sufferer for many years she was willing, nay impatient to go home to the Father. She said: "Time's up, let me rest a little and I will go on," and so painfully and consciously she closed her eyes in the sleep that knows no waking upon the shores of time, and her tired, troubled heart was at rest. An aged father and a brother and sister remain to mourn with the sorely bereaved husband and three sons the severing of one more earthly tie.

LEWIS EDWIN WALLING was born near Mt. Carmel, Ind., Sept. 23, 1850, and departed this life June 24, 1889, aged 38 years, 9 months and 1 day.

He was the son of Louis and Eliza Boyd Walling and a grandson of Rev. John Boyd. He was left at the age of sixteen without a mother's care

and went out to battle with life, determined to honor her memory by his worthy efforts. How successful he was, his many friends can testify. He was of a very amiable disposition and none knew him but to love him.

In 1881 he went to California. In 1882 he was married in San Francisco to Miss Etta Rafferty.

They lived near Inglenook, California, and it was on the morning of June 24th that he, in company with his brother-in-law, went to the mountain to haul, their team became frightened and he was thrown from the wagon and fatally injured. In a few hours he quietly passed over the boundary line between this life and the resting place of God's children, with the dying words: "I'm not afraid to die."

"Blessed are the dead who die in the Lord from henceforth. Yea, saith the spirit, that they may rest from their labors, and their works do follow them."

His funeral sermon was preached by Rev. J. S. Ross from Eccles. 12 ch., 1-7 verses.

And so year by year as we chronicle the passing away of one and another of our friends, let us confront each other with the thought that soon our toils and labors will be over and to us will come the

> "Crossing with abated breath and white set faces,
>   A little strip of sea,
> To find the loved ones waiting on the other shore,
> More beautiful, more precious than before."

NECROLOGY.

"BE YE ALSO READY."

Names.	Ob.	Generation.	Descendant of
Mrs. Jane Law,	10, 11, 1888,	9th,	Rev. James Boyd.
Mrs. Elizabeth Dickey,	12, 2, 1888,	3rd,	Mr. Robert Boyd.
Bennie Boyd,	1, 16, 1889,	5th,	Mr. Henry Boyd.
Mrs. Anna Boyd,	1, 18, 1889,	3rd,	Mr. Henry Boyd.
Mrs. Ellen Boyd,	3, 16, 1889,	4th,	Mr. Henry Boyd.
Mrs. Mary B. Black,	4, 16, 1889,	4th,	Mr. Henry Boyd.
Mr. Harvey Otterman,	6, 27, 1889,	5th,	Rev. Abraham Boyd.
Mrs. Mary Wilson,	8, 29, 1889,	3rd,	Mr. Henry Boyd.
Miss Sadie B. Negley,	9, 29, 1889,	5th,	Rev. Abraham Boyd.
Miss Myrtle Noble,	1889,	5th,	Mrs. Margt. B Shields.
Mrs. Sarah Agnes Graff,	11, 20, 1889,	5th,	Rev. James Boyd.
Lilian Boyd,	7, 30, 1888,	5th,	Rev. John Boyd.
Lewis E. Walling,	6, 24, 1889,	4th,	Rev. John Boyd.
M. Hillis Boyd,	7, 10, 1889,	4th,	Rev. Abraham Boyd.

MARRIAGES.

REPORTED SINCE PITTSBURGH REUNION.

Name.	Date.	Gen.	Descendant of
Orrin G. Boyd, Nora A. Murray.	11, 5, 1886.	5.	Henry Boyd.
Zillie Boyd, William Mading.	1, 30, 1880.	5.	Henry Boyd.
John Boyd Tamplin, Lettie ——— ———.	5, 2, 1889.	5.	Henry Boyd.
Frank Boyd Kemper, Ida J. Kleever.	11, 16, 1888.	5.	Henry Boyd.

BIRTHS.

REPORTED SINCE PITTSBURGH REUNION.

Albert Louis Darison,	7, 19, 1888,	6,	Henry Boyd.
Frederick L. Boyd,	11, 28, 1887,	6,	Henry Boyd.
Mary L. Boyd,	7, 6, 1889,	6,	Henry Boyd.
Ethel Boyd Kemper,	2, 12, 1889,	6,	Henry Boyd.
Bennie Boyd,	12, 23, 1888,	5,	Henry Boyd.

FOR THE BOYD REUNION, MARION, O.

BY REV. J. F. BOYD, STEUBENVILLE, O.

The highest praise be ever given
To Him who rules both earth and heaven,
   For all His wondrous love;
That here so many friends have come
Together in this harvest home,
   And hope to meet above.

More than a century has passed
Since great grandparent's lot was cast
   'Mid these wild western lands;
What hardships they did then endure!
But found God's grace was ever sure.
   When following His commands.

Praise ye the Lord, for covenant grace,
Which parents all do well to prove,
   And trust His promised grace;
"I'll be a God to thee and thine,
Supply their need by power divine,
   When they shall seek my face."

They'd daughters two and seven sons,
From each a line of kindred runs,
   With which few can compare;
And should the stream of life increase
Till earth shall suffer her decease
   Their history, who'll prepare?

God bless our kindred now on earth
With blessings of highest worth,
   Which any can enjoy,
That in their homes His praise shall sound,
And love and joy in all abound,
   His service their employ.

And when the last great trump shall sound,
To wake the dead wherever found,
   May all in glory rise!
And hail with joy our dearest Lord,
From Him receive the blest reward
   Forever in the skies.

O may we there each other greet,
And cast our crowns at Jesus' feet,
   And all His love extol,
With golden harps in sweetest strains,
'Mid heaven's bright, transporting plains,
   "And crown Him Lord of all."

MINUTES OF SESSION.

HOTEL MARION, August 27, 1890.

The members of the Boyd family met in their sixth reunion in the parlors of the Hotel Marion, according to previous announcement.

In the absence of the President the meeting was called to order by H. S. Smith. On motion R. G. Boyd was elected President, and Geo. J. Boyd, Secretary pro tem.

According to custom the convention joined in singing, "Blest be the Tie that Binds," after which prayer was offered by Abram Boyd.

The convention was welcomed to Marion by Miss Winona Hughes. Response by H. S. Smith.

After singing, "More Love to Thee, O Christ," the following committees were appointed:

1st. On time and place of next meeting: John E. Boyd, W. A. Wolf, H. S. Smith, J. W. Black, Miss Maggie Brown.

2nd. On resolution and death of M. Hillis Boyd: Mrs. S. C. Berryman, Mrs. Kate Minton, Miss Abigail E. Hill.

EVENING SESSION.

After being called to order, the convention joined in singing, "Jesus, Lover of My Soul," and were led in prayer by W. A. Wolf.

The convention was then favored with a couple of vocal selections by Miss Clara Richardson, daughter of "Mine Host."

Then followed an interesting history of Henry Boyd and descendants, by Mrs. S. C. Berryman, member of Historical Committee.

On motion it was decided to have the constitution published in each issue of convention report.

Committee to nominate officers: Kate Minton, Amanda Rose, Mattie Fye, Geo. J. Boyd, H. Steele Smith.

MORNING SESSION—AUGUST 28, 1890.

Devotional exercises conducted by the President.

Report of committees called for.

Committee on time and place of meeting reported in favor of Pittsburg, Pa., as place, and second week of September, 1892, as

time, and advised an adjourned meeting to be held in Chicago during the World's Fair, 1893. Report adopted.

Committee on Nomination of Officers reported as follows: President, Rev. T. S. Negley; Vice President, H. Steele Smith; Secretary and Treasurer, J. F. Wilson; Assistant Secretary, Geo. J. Boyd. Report adopted.

A large number of interesting communications from absent members were read by Mrs. S. C. Berryman.

Then devolved upon the Secretary the saddest part of the reunion—the reading of obituary notices.

Resolutions on death of M. Hillis Boyd were read, adopted, and ordered to be printed in minutes of Association.

H. Steele Smith was appointed to collect dues from all members of Association who were delinquent and forward same to Dr. J. F. Wilson.

Resolutions were adopted thanking Dr. J. F. Wilson for efficient services rendered Association; thanking Mr. A. S. Brown for roses forwarded convention; thanking "Mine Host" Richardson for courteous treatment to members of Association. These resolutions will be found in proper place in the proceedings of the convention.

On motion the secretary was instructed to publish in each report the names of members who paid their dues, the amount to be set opposite each name.

After singing "God be with You till We Meet Again," the convention was declared adjourned.   GEO. J. BOYD,
                                    Secretary pro tem.

RESOLUTIONS PASSED BY MARION REUNION.

1. We, the members of the Boyd family, wish to express our appreciation of the kindness of Mr. A. S. Brown in sending a remembrance of fragrant roses.

2. Vote of thanks to "Mine Host" Richardson for courteous treatment.

3. The Boyd Association meeting at Marion, August 28, 1890, return to Dr. Wilson, of Poulan, Georgia, a vote of their sincere thanks for his faithful labors in behalf of the Boyd Association, in his untiring efforts to promote the interest in said Association, and we sincerely hope he will be spared to continue his efficient services for many years.

LETTERS.

FAYETTE CITY, PA., August 23, 1890.

To the Boyd Kin:

I greet you in spirit, though absent in the body. I regret I must forego the pleasure of the warm greetings and hearty hand-shaking of you all.

The fellowship of the past reunions has whetted my appetite for more of just such sincere friendship and fellowship as these gatherings of kindred spirits afford. You know how hungry it makes you feel when you get the smell of the kitchen where delicious viands are being prepared and then are not privileged to sit down at the table where they are served. And our butler, Dr. Wilson, though his motive was no doubt a good one, has aggravated my appetite by sending me a *bill of fare*. What a feast you will have.

How we all will miss from our gatherings the familiar face of our inspiring leader, Hillis Boyd. But Hillis has gone to the reunion of the friends who have crossed the river, and to the assembly which *ne'er breaks up*. A couple of weeks ago I spent a day or two at his late home with his dear wife and children, and I trust the father's mantle is in some measure beginning all ready to fall upon the sons.

It seems to me that these reunions lead our thoughts, more than ever, to dear ones who have gone before and to the future fellowship we shall have with them. Our members are gradually crossing, and that our family record, without the blotting out of a single name, may be transferred to the Lamb's Book of Life, is my prayer.

With warmest feelings of affection we greet you all.

Yours in kindred bonds,

T. S. NEGLEY.

GREETING TO BOYD ASSOCIATION.

ST. CHARLES, August 21, 1890.

Dear Friends of the Boyd Reunion:

As I cannot be present with you at this meeting, I herewith send you one and all my heartfelt love and greetings of friendship, wishing that I could extend to you all the right hand and feel in reality that warmth of love that is in each heart of our kin. These friendly social gatherings are the green and fertile spots in the valley of life, to which memory will often recur in after years with pleasure. They tend to strengthen the bonds of sympathy, which should ever unite the hearts of kindred and friends.

Friends are but few on earth, and, therefore, dear, true friendship is my life, my joy. True friendship is something more than a name or a shadow; it soothes the sorrows and lightens the burdens of life; our meetings here will soon be o'er. Many since our last reunion have passed over to the reunion which never ends. May we all meet there!

I shall think of the reunion at Marion.

Your cousin,

S. A. HENRY.

MT. CARMEL, IND., August 18, 1890.

Dear Cousin:

I received your very kind invitation to visit you and attend the Boyd reunion, but it is with deep regret that I send you word that we cannot meet the friends in reunion at Marion, and not until this morning did we entirely give up going. But on account of ill health will have to forego the pleasure, and though absent in body, I am with you in spirit.

How I would like to be with you and look into the faces of the dear friends and feel the pressure of their hands; but snch is life—full of disappointments and sorrow. Since our last reunion death has again entered our family, taking a very near and dear brother—one of my twin brothers. Inclosed you will find his obituary, which we have neglected to send until now. Thus one by one we are passing over to join the innumerable company of God's ransomed ones. What a sweet reunion that will be.

May the Master bless you all, and may this be the most blessed meeting of all, is my prayer.

My husband and son join me in sending greeting and kindred love to all the friends. I remain as ever,

Your sincere cousin,

MARY A. BIDDINGS.

AKRON, OHIO, August 20, 1890.

Dear Friends of the Boyd Association:

I thank you for the invitation to be present at the reunion, and regret exceedingly that I cannot be with you on this occasion.

On the 30th of this month it will be a year since I have been confined to my room, and to my bed most of the time, by sickness, and at times suffer severe pain, yet I have very much to be thankful for—kind friends who sympathize with me in my affliction and do all they can to minister to my wants. I often think how sweet the rest will be when we reach the Beulah Land, where no sickness ever comes and God shall wipe away all tears from our eyes. I do not know how I could endure this long continued illness were it not that I feel the Great Physician near, and think over and over of the precious promises to those who put their trust in Him. Hoping to meet the dear ones who have gone before, with the kindred and friends who are journeying to the beautiful city where all is peace, I ask an interest in the prayer of the dear Christian friends of the convention that I may be *wholly* fitted for the Master's use, and my prayer is that we may hear the Father's, "Well done," when we reach the eternal shore.

Farewell, and "Blest be the tie that binds" our hearts in kindred Christian love.

I am not able to write, but send this by the hand of a friend.

Yours truly and affectionately,

MRS. ELIZA H. BOYD.

ELDORA, IOWA, Aug. 25, 1890.

To the Boyd Kin, in Convention assembled:

Up to within the past few days I had hoped to be present with you and renew some of the very happy associations among my kinsfolk in days gone by, and make others among those I have never had the pleasure of seeing.

I have seen but little of my kinsfolk for 33 years. I think your President when I last saw him was a "babe" in his mother's arms. But circumstances just now appear to prevent my going.

I wish you all a happy meeting, and still hope at some future time to meet with you.

       Truly Yours,   J. MITCHELL BOYD.

---

    437 LINDEN AVE., STEUBENVILLE, O., Aug. 11, 1890.

Dear Dr. Wilson:

This morning I received the programs of "The Boyd Reunion," and thank you for them. I am sorry that none of my family or I can go, for want of the necessary means. I have no place of preaching now—began over 37 years ago as a Home Missionary on a salary of $400, and for my whole life would not average over $500, and having children to educate, you will not think it strange that my purse is empty and no prospect of filling it. But we hope this "Reunion" will be the largest, most delightful and profitable.

You doubtless have received word of the death of our dear friend M. H. Boyd, Esq., near Freeport, Pa. I remember well of visiting at his father's, when a student. His grandmother and great-grandfather were then living near them. His great-grandfather, Craig, conducted family prayers in a manner that deeply impressed me. He seemed as an aged pilgrim already entered into Beulah Land." "Never saw him again; saw his grandmother a few times afterwards, and loved to hear her tell of the trials and scenes through which she had passed—dangers from the Indians, and scenes connected with the war of 1812-14.

His father and mother were very dear friends, humble, earnest, devoted christians; and two sisters, I remember, who died young. And now he is gone. I went to see him last May—a very pleasant visit, except very, very sorry to find him so ill; but hoped and prayed that he would be spared to his very interesting family. They have our deepest sympathy.

He was a man of most excellent spirit, a warm hearted friend, an humble and very devoted christian. In all my acquaintance with so many dear friends, I feel he was one of the best of men, and one of the best of christians. I trust that some one more nearly related and abler to do it will prepare a suitable and more extended sketch of his life and character.

What a happy reunion is gathering on the heavenly shore! It is delightful to contemplate!! What a blessed company is already there!

May the meeting in Marion be greatly blessed in bringing all nearer to the precious Savior, and to a sweeter, deeper experience of the love of God, that all may be better fitted for life's duties and trials, and for joining that blessed company before the throne!!

    "There my best friends, my kindred, dwell,
     There God, my Savior, reigns."

With kindest regards, and best wishes to you and family, and all the friends,

      Yours truly,   J. F. BOYD.

LaMoure, North Dakota, August 25, 1890.

Dear Kinsfolk and Cousins:

Though too far away to be bodily present with you in this reunion, yet swifter than the lightning, much swifter than these words are hurried to you, my *thought* darts right into the midst of your merry meeting, and almost literally enjoys some of its Boyd-like gladness in imagination beforehand and at this distance.

May this be a warm-hearted, happy occasion to you all, dear friends, as I am very sure it will be, though mellowed, as it must be, by the bodily absence of Cousin Hillis, translated since our last meeting to the still brighter company of that "part of the host" who "have crossed the flood." And when it comes our turn to pass beyond, may the same unerring blessed One who guided him, safely pilot us unto the celestial convention on the other shore, whose reunion never ends, but ever grows in joy and brightness while cycles run.

In faith and hope, and in sympathy for the bereft,

Your humble cousin,

J. S. BOYD.

Poulan, Ga., August 24, 1890.

To the Boyd Reunion, Marion, Ohio:

DEAR FRIENDS AND KINDRED:—My purpose was to attend every reunion of the Boyds, but I cannot, in justice to myself and business interests, be present at Marion.

I feel confident that you will have an enjoyable and profitable meeting, and trust that the Association—under its charter—may become well established and grow rapidly in favor and usefulness.

Wishing you all the full measure of kindred enjoyment, I am,

Very truly yours,

J. F. WILSON.

Tarentum, Pa., August 23, 1890.

Dear Friends:

When I received the circular from our Secretary, announcing the time and place of our next meeting, I thought it might be that I could be present, but more recently, affliction has come to our home and some of us have been weakened so that we find it impossible to be present, and I trust that you all will have a pleasant and profitable time.

Love to all the friends and kindred of the Boyd family in reunion at Marion. Sincerely,

MRS. THOS. MILLER.

Tarentum, Allegheny Co., Pa.

Allegheny, Pa., August 23, 1890.

Dear Friends of the Boyd Association:

Compliments and congratulations to all the dear friends of the Boyd Association.

I feel that words cannot express my sorrow in not being able to attend our reunion in Marion, Ohio.

What pleasant recollections I have of our meeting in Pittsburgh, and how often have I tried to recall the names of those faces that appear on memory's walls, and how often have I thought if the meetings of friends on earth are so pleasant and joyous, what must that reunion beyond be like, "Where congregations ne'er break up and Sabbaths have no end."

Please extend to all our dear friends in reunion my sincere love and kindred greeting.

As ever, very truly and sincerely,
MRS. JULIA A. SCOTT.
167 Arch St., Allegheny City, Pa.

FREEPORT, August 23, 1890.

Mr. R. G. Boyd:

DEAR COUSIN:—Enclosed you will find a list of deaths—my own dear husband one of the number. His death is a great loss to me, but we must not complain, for God knows best.

Please remember me to all the friends that you will meet at the reunion. The children and I feel very lonely. Love from all to all.

Your cousin,
LIZZIE F. BOYD.

WICHITA, KANS., August 14, 1890.

J. F. Wilson, Esq., Poulan, Ga.:

DEAR SIR:—The notice of the Boyd reunion, to be held at Marion, Ohio, on August 27th and 28th next, is received. While it would afford me no little pleasure to be present at the reunion and participate in the diatetic as well as the social festivities of so interesting a convention as I am led to believe this will be, and while I fully appreciate the social pleasure of meeting face to face so numerous a kith and kin, still a large and urgent practice here in a profession which brooks no substitute, and excuses no neglect, obliges me to forego the pleasure of being one of the merry-makers in the gala occasion of August 27-28.

But while I shall be absent in person, believe me, I shall be present in spirit and well-wishes, moving among you, as it were, and eager to grasp the extended hand of those who are bound to me by the sanguine ties of a brotherhood true as gold and lasting as the hills.

I shall ever hold myself in readiness to do what I can towards promoting the best interests of the organization, in which membership is an honor, and which numbers among its members so many honorable, eminent and knightly representatives; both in the civil as well as in the professional and literary walks of life.

Wishing you, therefore, a most successful, pleasant and joyous reunion, I have the honor to be,

Fraternally yours,
B. Y. BOYD, M. D.

TREASURER'S REPORT.

The Treasurer's report for two years ending Aug. 25th, 1890, was among the papers that failed to reach the Marion Reunion.

The following abstract from the cash book will serve to give an idea of the accounts at that date:

Receipts.

Cash on hand Sept. 6, 1888	$ 2 80
Received dues from members	49 00
" from sale of Pamphlets	4 40
" " " Records	7 50
	$63 70

Expenses.

Paid balance due Treasurer from 1886	$ 12 44
" amount advanced by H. S. Smith	3 00
" Incorporation expenses	16 40
" for 500 Announcements of Marion Reunion	2 75
" " 500 Programs for Marion Reunion	3 50
" " 300 Pamphlets Pittsburg Reunion	71 30
" " 300 copies Fraternal Letter	1 50
" " Envelopes and Stationery	1 80
" " Freight and express on Pamphlets	2 43
" " Postage	6 77
	$121 89
Balance due Treasurer	58 19

J. F. WILSON, *Treas.*

Poulan, Ga., Aug. 23, 1890.

REPORT OF COMMITTEE ON INCORPORATION.

To The Boyd Association:

Your committee appointed in 1888 to secure the incorporation of the Boyd Association reports the accomplishment of duty assigned, and herewith present charter and record book showing the regular and full organization under the corporation laws of Ohio.

Soliciting approval of our work and desiring to be discharged if same is approved, we respectfully submit,

1st.—A certified copy of articles of incorporation.

2nd.—A record of organization under said charter.

3rd.—The certificates of five trustees, who were duly qualified.

[Signed.]   J. F. WILSON,
            Chairman of Committee.

Poulan, Ga., Aug. 23, 1890.

CORPORATION.

In response to a call of the committee appointed at Pittsburg reunion, a meeting was held at Marion, Ohio, the 26th and 27th of September, 1888, and the business completed as far as practicable.

The following is an abstract from records of the Incorporation as far as written:

STATE OF OHIO.

These Articles of Incorporation of The Boyd Association

Witnesseth, That we, the undersigned, all of whom are citizens of the State of Ohio, desiring to form a corporation—not for profit—under the general corporation laws of said State,

Do Hereby Certify, First, The name of said corporation shall be The Boyd Association.

Second. Said corporation shall be located and its principal business transacted at Marion, in Marion county, Ohio.

Third. The purposes for which said corporation is formed are:

1st.—The collecting, publishing and distribution of historical reminiscences of the family of John and Mary Fulton Boyd.

2nd—The maintaining and strengthening of family ties among the descendants of said John and Mary Fulton Boyd.

3rd—The occasional convening of said kindred in family reunions.

In Witness Whereof We have hereto set our hands this twenty-sixth day of September, A. D. 1888.

ROBERT G. BOYD,
JAMES F. WILSON,
EZEKIEL HUGHES,
J. E. HUGHES,
PATRICK H. OTIS.

THE STATE OF OHIO, } ss.
COUNTY OF MARION,

On the 26th day of September, A. D. 1888, personally appeared before me, the undersigned, a Notary Public within and for said county, the above named Robert G. Boyd, James F. Wilson, Ezekiel Hughes, J. E. Hughes and Patrick H. Otis, who each severally acknowledged the signing the foregoing articles of incorporation to be his free act and deed, for the uses and purposes therein mentioned.

Witness my hand and official seal on the day and year last aforesaid.

{ SEAL. }

MARCUS B. CHASE,
Notary Public,
Marion County, Ohio.

THE STATE OF OHIO, } ss.
COUNTY OF MARION,

I, Harry R. Young, Clerk of Court of Common Pleas within and for the county aforesaid, do hereby certify that Marcus B. Chase, whose name is subscribed to the foregoing acknowledgement as a Notary Public, was at the date thereof a Notary Public in and for said county, duly commissioned and qualified and authorized to take said acknowledgement, and further, that I am well acquainted with his handwriting and believe that the signature to said acknowledgement is genuine.

In Witness Whereof I have hereunto set my hand and seal of said court at Marion this 26th day of September, A. D. 1888.

HARRY R. YOUNG,
Clerk.

{ SEAL. }

UNITED STATES OF AMERICA, }
    STATE OF OHIO,
    Office of the Secretary of State. }

I, J. S. Robinson, Secretary of State of the State of Ohio, do hereby certify that the foregoing is a true copy, carefully compared by me with the original, now in my legal custody as Secretary of State, and found to be true and correct, of the articles of incorporation of The Boyd Association filed in this office on the 26th day of September, A. D. 1888, and recorded in Vol. 37, page 541, of Records of Incorporations.

In Testimony Whereof I have hereunto subscribed my name and affixed my official seal, at Columbus, this 27th day of September, A. D. 1888.   J. S. ROBINSON,

Secretary of State.

{ SEAL. }

WAIVER OF NOTICE.

We, the undersigned, being all the incorporators of The Boyd Association, and this day personally present at Marion, do hereby waive the giving of notice of the first meeting of said Association, and direct that the same be held this day at 4 o'clock P. M. at the residence of the said Ezekiel Hughes, in said town of Marion, Ohio. Witness our signatures this 27th day of September, 1888.

ROBERT G. BOYD,
JAMES F. WILSON,
EZEKIEL HUGHES,
J. E. HUGHES,
PATRICK H. OTIS,
Incorporators.

MARION, OHIO, Sept. 27th, 1888.

In accordance with provisions of Waiver of Notice of Incorporators, for first meeting of The Boyd Association, a meeting of members and Incorporators was held.

The Constitution of the Association, as adopted at Lima con-

vention in 1883, was re-adopted as a basis for a constitution under the charter, and amendments offered which would provide for a board of six trustees—two to be elected annually and serve for a term of six years.

It was provided that meetings of Association be regularly held in the early autumn of each alternate year.

J. F. Wilson was appointed to draft a revised constitution and submit the same for consideration of Association at its next regular meeting.

Trustees were elected as follows:

Robert G. Boyd and James F. Wilson, with term to expire in 1890; R. D. Humes and A. Fulton Boyd, with term to expire in 1892; Joseph F. Boyd and Chas. N. Boyd, with term to expire in 1894. Meeting then adjourned.

R. G. BOYD,
    Chairman.

J. F. WILSON,
    Acting Secretary.

QUALIFICATIONS OF TRUSTEES.

STATE OF PENNSYLVANIA, } ss.
COUNTY OF WESTMORELAND. }

Personally appeared before me, a Justice of the Peace in and for said county, Capt. R. D. Humes, who, being duly sworn according to law, deposes and says: That he was duly elected a Trustee of The Boyd Association, and that he is willing to serve and act as Trustee of said Association.
    R. D. HUMES.

Sworn to and subscribed before me this 18th day of June A. D. 1889.
    G. W. WASHABAUGH,
    Justice of the Peace.

To Whom it may Concern:

In the matter of The Boyd Association, incorporated under the laws of the State of Ohio, the undersigned, being appointed one of the Trustees of said Association, promises to faithfully and conscientiously perform the duties of the office to the best of his ability.
    [Signed.]
    C. N. BOYD.

STATE OF PENNSYLVANIA, } ss.
COUNTY OF BUTLER. }

On this 22nd day of June, A. D., 1889, before me, a Notary Public duly sworn and commissioned in and for said State and county, personally came C. N. Boyd, above named trustee, who, being duly sworn, deposes and

says that he will diligently and faithfully perform the duties of above appointment with all fidelity to the best of his ability. C. N. BOYD.
Sworn and subscribed before me this day and year aforesaid.

A. W. CORNELIUS,
[SEAL.] Notary Public.

POLAND, OHIO, July 15th, 1889.

I Hereby Certify That The Boyd Association, formed some eight years ago for the purpose of perpetuating the history of John and Mary Fulton Boyd and their descendants, at its last meeting, held at the city of Pittsburgh, Pa., in the fall 1888, directed its Secretary to organize and have sworn into office a Board of Trustees for the purpose of receiving moneys in legacies and otherwise to meet the necessary expenses of said history.

I also certify that the Secretary of said Association, Dr. J. F. Wilson, requests that I be sworn in as a member of said Board of Trustees.

A. FULTON BOYD.

Personally appeared before me, a Notary Public in and for Poland township, and was duly sworn in as a member of said Board of Trustees, as above named, this 15th day of July, 1889.

J. H. DAVIDSON,
[SEAL.] Notary Public.

THE STATE OF OHIO, } ss.
MARION COUNTY. }

I, R. G. Boyd, do solemnly swear that I will, to the best of my ability and understanding, discharge the various duties of Trustee of The Boyd Association, to which I have been appointed, and for so long a time as I shall hold said trust, and until my successor has been appointed and qualified. R. G. BOYD.

Sworn to before me by R. G. Boyd and by him subscribed in my presence this 24th day of July, A. D. 1889.

JOHN A. WALFORD.
Notary Public.

GEORGIA, } ss.
WORTH COUNTY. }

Personally appeared before me, the undersigned, a duly appointed and qualified Justice of the Peace in and for said county, James F. Wilson, who was sworn by me according to law to faithfully, impartially, and to the best of his ability, to perform the duties incumbent upon him as a Trustee of The Boyd Association, a corporation existing under the laws of the State of Ohio.

In testimony thereof I have hereunto affixed my name, at Poulan, in said State of Georgia, this 4th day of November, A. D. 1889.

JAMES F. WILSON.

W. H. LANCASTER,
    N. P., ex-O. J. P.

REPORT OF SPECIAL COMMITTEE ON CONSTITUTION FOR THE BOYD ASSOCIATION.

PREAMBLE.—The descendants of John and Mary Fulton Boyd, of the third, fourth and fifth generations, being desirous of promoting friendship, love and esteem of kindred, and hoping to combine efforts in gathering incidents of family history and in making permanent records of the political, social, industrial and religious influence of its members, and thus striving to create a more earnest desire to emulate the virtues of a Godly ancestry, have associated themselves for these and kindred purposes, under authority of the State of Ohio, and hereby adopt the following Constitution for regulating and perpetuating its purposes:

ARTICLE I.—NAME.

SECTION 1. This organization shall be known as "THE BOYD ASSOCIATION."

SEC. 2. The official headquarters of the corporation shall be at Marion, Ohio.

ARTICLE II.—OF WHOM COMPOSED.

SECTION 1. Any descendant of John and Mary Fulton Boyd, or any person to whom such descendant shall have been lawfully married, or any adopted child of any such descendant, may become a member of this Association by complying with the requirements of members.

SEC. 2. The membership of this Association shall be composed of: 1st.—Life members. 2nd.—Active members. 3rd.—Corresponding members.

ARTICLE III.—MEETINGS.

SECTION 1. Regular meetings of this Association shall be held biennally at such date and place as may be duly appointed.

SEC. 2. Special meetings may be called when in the judgment of Trustees and officers it is deemed necessary or expedient.

SEC. 3. Auxiliary meetings may be held under supervision of Association as circumstances will permit.

SEC. 4. In all regular meetings of Association one-fifth the active membership, in person or by proxy, shall constitute a quorum for the transaction of business.

ARTICLE IV.—OFFICERS.

SECTION 1. The officers of this Association shall consist of a board of six Trustees, two of whom shall be elected at each regular biennial meeting and serve for a term of six years, or until their successors are elected and qualified.

Sec. 2. A President, Vice President, Scribe and Treasurer shall be elected biennially at regular meeting.

Sec. 3. A Historical Committee of nine members shall be elected for a term of six years, with term of but three members of same to expire at same meeting.

Sec. 4. A Statistical Committee of three members, to serve a term of six years, one to be elected at each biennial meeting.

ARTICLE V.—Duties of Officers.

Section 1. It shall be the duty of Trustees to receive and duly account for all property, moneys, legacies, bequests or other valuables received by, accruing to, or donated to the Association, and to use such property in such ways as may best subserve the purposes for which said funds were collected. They shall make a biennial report of all matters engaging their attention as such Trustees.

Sec. 2. The President and Vice President and Scribe shall perform such duties as usually belong to their respective offices, and shall—with such assistants as may be duly appointed—arrange for, conduct and publish proceedings of biennial and auxiliary meetings.

Sec. 3. The Treasurer shall be the custodian of all moneys and property, disbursing the same only upon the written order of trustees. He shall give bond in such amount as may be from time to time required by the Board of Trustees for the faithful performance of his duties.

Sec. 4. The Historical Committee shall collect, preserve, and, as authorized by Trustees, publish matter of historical and biographical interest to the kin. They shall report work accomplished at each biennial meeting.

Sec. 5. The Statistical Committee shall maintain, correct and build the family record, and make biennial reports of all deaths, marriages and births accruing in the family during such period.

ARTICLE VI.—Duties of Members.

Section 1. It shall be the duty of all members of this Association to labor by precept and example to maintain the sterling characteristics of an honored ancestry.

Sec. 2. They shall co-operate with the officers in all laudable efforts to accomplish the purposes of this Association.

Sec. 3. They shall pay such dues as are respectively required by this Constitution of the different classes of members.

ARTICLE VII.—Dues and Privileges of Members.

Section 1. The payment of one hundred dollars, in such installments as may be ordered by trustees, shall constitute a life membership. Such members shall receive duplicate copies of all publications and family records issued by Association, and enjoy all the privileges granted other classes of membership.

Sec. 2. The payment of one dollar biennially and signing the Constitution shall constitute active membership. Such members shall receive one

copy of each publication issued, and have a right to vote in person or by proxy at all regular and special meetings. On failure to pay biennial dues for two successive reports of Treasurer, such membership may be transferred to the corresponding members class.

Sec. 3. The payment of one or more dollars (with no biennial dues) shall constitute a corresponding member. Such members shall be entitled to receive a copy of all notices and announcements, same as active and life members, and copy of any publication issued by Association at cost of same.

ARTICLE VIII.—Amendments.

This Constitution may be amended or changed by the consent thereto of two-thirds the active and life members, at any regular meeting of the Association. Respectfully submitted,

J. F. Wilson,
Special Committee.

ROLL OF VISITORS AT MARION.

1. Byers, Carrie L., Prospect, O.
2. Ginsley, Mrs. T. H., Marion, O.
3. Jones, Mary M., Lima, O.
4. Landon, John, Marion, O.
5. Uline, G. W., Washington, D. C.
6. Wright, Geo. H., Marion, O.
7. Wright, Mrs. Mattie C., Marion, O.

NEW MEMBERS OF ASSOCIATION.

J. Mitchell Boyd,
Miss S. Lina Boyd,
Mrs. Jane H. Boyd,
Miss Flora Boyd,
Mrs. Kate Minton.
Mrs. Mary Van Houtan.
Mrs. Sarah J. Boyd,
Miss Fannie A. Boyd,
Miss I. Jennie Boyd,
Miss Abigail Hill,
Mrs. Sallie M. O'Neil.
Miss A. Lizzie Boyd,
Howell M. Boyd,
Miss Lizzie Boyd,
Thos. R. Hughes.
Mrs. M. A. Rose.
W. A. Wolf.

ROLL OF MARION REUNION.

1. Berryman, Miss Myrtle, Lima, O.
2. Berryman, Mrs. S. C., Lima, O.
4. Boyd, Abraham, Lima, O.
5. Boyd, Miss I. Jennie, Black Hawk, Pa.
6. Boyd, Mrs. Flora E., Marion, O.
7. Boyd, John, Criderville, O.
8. Boyd, John E., Allegheny, Pa.
9. Boyd, George J., Black Hawk, Pa.
10. Boyd, Sallie C., Lima, O.
11. Boyd, R. G., Marion, O.
12. Brown, Mrs. Maggie E., South Oil City, Pa.
13. Codding, Mrs. Clara B., Woodland, O.
14. Codding, L. R., Woodland, O.
15. Codding, Boyd, Woodland, O.
16. Codding, Bessie, Woodland, O.
17. Fye, Mrs. Mattie, St. Charles, O.
20. Harkins, Mrs. Lizzie, Marion, O.
19. Harkins, Hugh H., Marion, O.
18. Fye, Mrs. Mary J., St. Charles, O.
21. Hughes, Mrs. J. E., Marion, O.
22. Hughes, E., Marion, O.
23. Hughes, Miss Maggie E., Marion, O.
24. Hughes, Miss Winona A., Marion O.
25. Hughes, Thos. R., Marion, O.
26. Hill, Miss Abigail E., Freeport, Pa.
27. Minton, Mrs. Kate, Mellville, O.
28. O'Neil, Mrs. Sallie M., Berlin Centre, O.
29. Otis, Mrs. Sarah A., Kenton, O.
30. Otis, Joseph Fulton, Kenton, O.
31. Otis, Mattie A., Kenton, O.
32. Otis, Rebecca, Kenton, O.
33. Rose, Mrs. M. Amanda, Palmyra, O.
34. Smith, H. S., Freeport, Pa.
35. Van Houten, M. B., Marion, O.
36. Van Houten, Chas. Marion, O.
37. Wolf, W. A. Criderville, O.
38. Wolf, Mrs. M. B. Criderville, O.

BOOK READY.

NAME:

The Lost Ship and the Saved Tribe;
OR,
The Boyds and Their Kin,

AND OTHER POEMS.

Author,
REV. JAMES SHIELDS BOYD,
LaMoure, North Dakota.

DESCRIPTION.—Contains 124 pages; printed on good paper; press work excellent; well bound; neatly lettered. Five illustrations: 1. Likeness of author. 2. Ship leaving an Erin port. 3. Rustic church in American forest. 4. Likeness of M. Hillis Boyd. 5. The duck hunters. Pieces of Music: 1. The Praise and Hope of Kindred. 2. Our Christmas Ship. 3. Little Girl and Her Canary.

CONTENTS.—1. Boyd Convention Poems: One read at Beaver, Pa., October, 1881; one read at Lima, Ohio, October, 1883. 2. In Memoriam Verses: Three brothers, mother, father, Cousin Hillis Boyd, to whom all the Boyds and their kin owe much, and whose memory all fondly cherish; Garfield, and several poems addressed to parishoners in affliction. 3. Miscellany. Sixteen brief, off-hand poems, grave and gay, on a variety of subjects.

PRICE.—One dollar and twenty-five cents ($1.25) per copy. Sent by mail on receipt of price. Address all orders as above to

J. S. BOYD,
, LaMoure, North Dakota.

NOTE—The cost of cuts (photo engravings and music plates), the limited field the book will have for circulation (being largely of a *family* and *personal* nature), make it necessary to fix the price named, in order to meet expenses of publication.

www.ingramcontent.com/pod-product-compliance
Lightning Source LLC
Chambersburg PA
CBHW031605110426
42742CB00037B/1235